Pick a Pet

Contents

What Pet?	2
Dogs	6
Cats	8
Hamsters	10
Stick Insects	12
Fish	14

Written by Sarah Loader

What Pet?

You might like a pet that you can take out, or one that stays in.

You might think a big pet is fun,
or you might like a little one.

Whichever pet you like,
they all need food, drink ...

... and a good spot to rest.

Dogs

Dogs come in all shapes. Some are big and some are little.

All dogs need to go out.
They like to play with you!

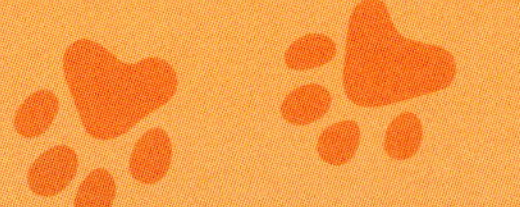

Cats

If cats have a cat flap, they can do as they wish. They can go out to play, or come in and rest.

Cats sleep a lot.

Hamsters

Hamsters are little and soft. They can be held but do not let them escape!

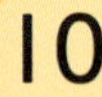

Hamsters sleep all day and do not need to go out.

They like to run in a wheel at night.

Stick Insects

You do not need a shop to get stick insect food. They like twigs and plants from the garden or a park.

Stick insects do not play, but they are fun to spot!

Fish

Fish can swim in a tank and in a pond.
They might be bright or plain.

You can pop lots of things in their tanks
to make it fun for them.

Pick the best pet for you!